Before the Fall

A Book of Poetry

Vasilios I. Vitogiannis

Warning: the following poems are totally full of shit, and if you actually read them all, there must be something seriously wrong with you."

Other Books by Vasilios I. Vitogiannis:

Somewhere In Between

RESURRECTION

The FOURTH Of Its KIND

If you would like to find us on Social Media

please check out our website:

http://www.upliftinghumanity.net

Table of Contents

A Befuddled Moth 1

An Unending Ceiling of *Feeling* 3

Aspects of Self 5

Body positioned 6

Brief Hallucination 7

Dearest 8

Desire for Descent 10

Deva Stated 12

Devout Archaeologists 13

DNA 15

Every Friday, the Garbage Guy 16

Flatter Me...Again 18

From Tusk Till Dawn 19

Gentle Twinkle 21

Gleaming Gray 22

Golgotha 23

I can't help but wonder 27

I understand if you miss me, Michael 30

If This Makes Sense to You You're On Crack... Or In Love 32

Imaginary Time 34

In a Ballroom 35

Karma 36

Knowledge Has No Ledge 37

Little Poetry Bio 39

Lying with Purpose 40

Midstream 41

Miss Chief 42

My Friend.. 43

My Heart Is Rewiring My Brain 45

Nursed Back to Wealth 46

Occurrence in a Saloon, 3:30 p.m. 47

Oh the things we can do 48

Oh, the poet! 49

On His Quest 50

One Candle Brings Its Light to Many More 52

Orders from Within.. 53

Peek-a-Boo 55

Pioneer of Acrobatics 56

Raven, Raven, Raven 58

Road Trip 59

Roadkill 61

Rocks 62

Save the Piano for Tomorrow 63

School Will Not Prepare You 65

Shedding Stalactites 66

She's There 68

Silence 70

Somewhere Out There 71

Space and Time Fall for Each Other 72

Stay Away From Lucy's Forest 74

Stitching a Star 76

Tanning 78

That Which Will Not Bear a Name... 80

The Created Also Creates the Creator 81

The French 82

The Horse Will Ride 83

The Lady Bugs, A Mad Man 84

The Plant Kingdom 86

The Quicker Route 87

The Sighs of A House Cat 88

The Tragic Comedian... 89

There's an angel in your eyes that I'd love for you to see. 91

Thirteen 92

Thoughts From Behind a Body 93

Three Polka Dots in a Jazz bar 94

Travel 96

Two Lips Like Tulips 97

Unbothered 98

What if There Were An Ersatz Elevator 99

When the Moon is Full 101

Why Else 102

Why? 104

With Lover's Eyes 105

Wonder and Wander 107

Your Hair in the Wind 109

A Befuddled Moth

The chemistry of my brain,

tinkered with by no inexperienced chemist

cruising in the laboratory,

ford's full of exploratory

the day Dora became oratory,

this means through the ears – audio

those things that bounce up and around

like infinitesimal drums reverberating of their own accord

within a postulating *cul-de-sac* -

I always thought that word sounded like ballsack – anyway,

away from kindergarten,

off to fertile winter garden

where the warden is both Warren and Guardian

and the staff he holds upright

is none other than the Bass Clef, hooked sideways

like a lobster gazing at you lopsidedly.

Please! Please don't eat me senor. I'm still alive in this fucking lobster
tank at a Chinese joint.

How many food hubs do you need to satisfy you?

I'll take Mediterranean over Indian any day.

That's cuz the latter is a volcano

when the fireman descending

fumbles his keys, tumbles his G's, and falls

flat onto his face in C Minor,

Bach would be *so upset.*

I haven't come up yet,

I'm still on Earth dummy.

Here where the moths bump repeatedly into windowpanes

fulfilling their own appointed *Quests of the Light,*

we call them *Legends-In-Their-Own-Minds*;

Well why don't you tell somebody about it? *Make the inert*

physical.

Well duh!

Why the hell do you think

I'm sitting here bumpin' into this window right in front of you!

Open it for me. Help a brotha out.

I says why are you speaking in a black accent?

I am quite obviously dark, and seek to balance my outward

abundance of fluctuating melanin with a more substantial

radiant being.

Fine.

I opened the window

and the moth flew straight into my eyes.

An Unending Ceiling of *Feeling*

Once upon a dime,

or the lack of it,

there was an entourage of gypsies

in a man,

the holiest Sabbaths

of reckless auto-tune

and Duran Duran.

He ran he ran,

not to a place,

but for the solace of being

in all of Space.

Every table and countertop -

I'll whip the whip

and counter-talk,

Why would time speed?

repeatedly asked,

by the witch whose witch whose witch;

the reason for their seasonal laughs

and rhythmic cackles of the throat are had

at the vocalist's expense,

where synergy's dense,

Before the fall

and happenstance

was his perverted (and as he flirted)

worded,

romance.

But the mole be-fixed a-twixt the witch

and her begotten, rotten smile

were all the while a means to pitch

her efforts up against the tile

and no,

she was not a ceiling.

Aspects of Self

Musician

Joker

Teacher

Seer

Shaman

Healer

Lover

Warrior

Loner

Anxious Girl

Boy seeking his Manhood

Mermaid

Tarzan

Nomad

Dancer

Intellectual

Mad Scientist

Wise One

Boy enwrapped in Fantasy

All these things,

he was all these things

and goodness knows how many more

Body positioned

Body positioned,
Location Locked.
I've been gone,
that's why you knocked.
When I don't answer,
you'll be upset.
My body's here,
My mind not yet.

Brief Hallucination

Creaking, shrieking,

the Kraken, wreaking

atrocities in a city,

like a Giant Black Transformer,

only to be seduced by an old lady wearing white,

and *subdued*

by a man wearing an earl gray tuxedo.

His rope is,

from chest hair to chest hair

enwrapped by bosom, *enraptured*

by a twosome,

this between old lady

and buffalo bronco man.

What do buffaloes have to do with it?

Well,

they graze around

and can organize a hell of a stampede.

Ah yes, remarked the old man telling this story,

That's where I've put my drugs.

Dearest

My dear,

I feel you in my bones.

You are the synapse through which my neurons connect.

The axon and our fairy tale, like dendrites sprouting from the source.

A pond of water so deep it takes place in your eyelids.

I'm not sure what you're looking at; it's probably a reflection.

As you cast the lifelong shadow upon yourself, The Man

Equipped With The Solar Furnace

is prompted to find you, to carry you, to haunt you.

Your warmth begs his beauty.

I am there with you.

Now, please tell the kids to shut off the lights before they go to bed.

They might not want to see a father crippled

by lack of anxiety and a head in the clouds.

They could only fathom the depths

from which we sprang like a lily,

revealing itself to you in a myriad of ways,

each one thicker – brighter – than the last.

'N still you twirled it, hand in hand,

fixated by a stem which grew into a vein,

Billy

the median vein into your left hand -

there where the cells regenerate because of it

and everything you have done and are doing up to this point.

Your unicellular tissues an ode

to kids with stuffy noses

and stubbing their toes.

Desire for Descent

Without warning

the rose is thorning

leaving, heaving, grieving sighs

and *I wonder, wonder why's*

all beneath sunkist umbrellas and white water rapids

of commonplace despair

a plumber with no keys to spare

trying locks discouragedly and grimacing

in public view and widespread opinion

the pigs going *oink* even in death

with their wafty souvenirs of smell

a carcass temporarily resurrected

by some bow and arrow

the bone and marrow, skin alike

upturned snout

and four legs that would stammer

all about, occasionally rearing on its hind legs

buried carelessly to the loins

in a trough of stagnant mud-water

home to mosquitoes, their eggs

and parasitic electricities

slashing through hydrogen at the molecular level

Billy

and the oxygen left stranded

in its O shape

a phosphorescent strobe light

apparition

its feet dangling

off the crepuscular edge of a crescent moon

no shoes, whistling

ruminating with the breeze

in between its toes

as to how and why it is so glad

that its shoes should be missing

at a time like this.

Deva Stated

Deva Stated
and Whis purred
while his ex claims
were ignored;
and the chairs wanted the tables
to re-spawn directly
to their author. Itty
bitty spy dares
present
in the Phallus tin Ian uses
to measure plural pleasures
that are REM in isn't
of rose cess flow, worrying
about weather
or not
double entendres mean squat
another four teen pounds
or wait, lifting;
real lice sing
that 11 ups has 4 more downs
than any seven could ever mustard.

Devout Archaeologists

When I would play

with ice and fire, I remember

every time they would collide

the unseen chemical acrobatics

approaching, circling, repelling

just enough.

How they kept up

their transcendent waltz

in a neutral ballroom, the lights

usually fading

usually fa...

The little pyre would grab the icy torso

and insinuate, *in sin you ate,*

Come,

Come and burn, with *me,*

Before the fall

Let's spread, and spread

What's dead?

What's dead.

Instead,

the ice withdrew

unto its hollow cavern, huddled

watching the water drip

from the melting stalactites

and they discovered remnants underneath the thawing eons

in that wall

of hieroglyphics

of men

of bonfires

of *bond* fires

and a twirl

of stampeding jungle men

riveted

by the transfer of heat.

DNA

He had written it down verbatim
and then... silence.
Silence as the blueprint was enacted,
or was it perhaps a red hobgoblin?
smorgasbord of cylindrical helixes
wont to intertwine with one another,
murmuring at the cornerstone,
where stem meets stalk,
where phlegm meets hawk
and spat out expeditiously,
the remnants of the dribble sectioned off
in the eyes of the beholder.
Be. Hold her.
You are absolutely stunning, tonight,
here, in your black gown
and I watch the way it drapes you,
like two silhouettes becoming one
in the moonlight.

Every Friday, the Garbage Guy

Channeling energy into words
is quite the endeavor;
I'm sure it might be something like birth.

Woah!
There goes the human head
out of the vagina,
crowning in its passage,
clowning the doctors
like a set of well-meaning jesters
welcoming this new soul.

"Hey buddy," they say.
"What's your name?"

God
how quick we are
to define something,
to classify it;
store it in one of those useless folders
of our mental filing cabinets.

The brain is literally
any sane man's nightmare,

Billy

crammed with papers
and *Whose Line Is It Anyway* trivia.

Thank god (who?)
there is a content garbage-truck driver
that stops by every Friday,
disposing of your trash
while whistling his life away.

Flatter Me...Again

How many times will we undress before the Ferris wheel?
Or how about,
the number of times the operator pats us on the shoulder,
yet gently shoves us toward our designated trolley?

Buckle Up.

This is something he says to you,
and in that moment when you are suspended
at 12 o'clock, top of the wheel,
you will squeal as *déjà vu*
casts its clutches over you,
as each revolution will reveal
the orange *(last time)* you forgot to peel.

From Tusk Till Dawn

Undress me horizontally.
I welcome your buzzing about like a busy bee.
Pollinate me. Keep being predictable.
Then wing around, selfish
to the next object of your nature,
(desirably) to carry on stampeding
the emphatic vistas
of the humanity confined to a sunflower.

It's your fault you have a stinger.

Evolution is the ball in your court,
sounding out its dribbles
in parades of gay pride
and the spittle of lispy syllables.
You.
Yeah, you.
Don't jog. Run!
to your pen silly
and tell Usain Bolt during his comedown
how similarly willy-nilly elephants
are to handicapped hyenas.
Of course the tusks chose their protrusion

Before the fall

in their charity-supported effort to portrait an illusion

As if anything had any free will,

ever.

Gentle Twinkle

There is a man who dines alone
sleeps alone,
dresses the same.
Takes long walks
through crowded city streets,
sips his tea,
alone.
Don't get me wrong,
it's not the bad kind of alone;
this solitude is his greatest tool
and he knows it.
It's funny how the food starts tasting better,
the women smell more strongly,
his footsteps less audible.
He knows, by now
how to go unnoticed
by the majority
but how to richly touch the souls he meets,
then leave a gentle twinkle in the eyes
of those who see.

Gleaming Gray

My woman of passive fancy,
passion of darkest night -
where has the time gone?

The edges of your silhouette
wrapped up in your night gown,
your teeth
clicking like clocks with excitement

The remnants of an autumn breeze
falling by your floundering knees,
like Nemo the fish in an orange headdress
as I make room to peel back your heart from your head

Boy,
you were orange when I left you,
and here,
it is here I feel
like a nuanced shade of gray proclaiming itself to you

teeth gleaming like candles
as you frolic about the marketplace,
eyes gleaming like glowsticks
when you want them to.

Golgotha

Once upon a time, there was a boy.
Inside this boy was a girl.
She did not weigh much –
the equivalent of several feathers, *maybe*.

She was constantly taking flight inside him;
using the clay that was his body,
she was constantly taking form.

He loved her presence and the presents therefrom.
He had to learn to listen to her.

She was very soft-spoken
and it took quite a bit of training
to receive her whispers.
One could not hear her
over the vacuum
of a constantly churning mind.
Did I mention how constantly things were happening?

All the time, she loved him.
It just so happened that one day,
as he was preparing to head for bed
(in reality he slept on the floor;

he was never fond of the too-accommodating beds),
he happened to catch a glimpse of herself,
I mean *himself,*
in the mirror.

He didn't know what to say.
As if reading his thoughts,
like a fairy godmother,
she politely responded:
There's nothing you need to say.

By now he was perplexed.
It was a nice confusion though.
It almost felt pleasurable to be in his skin
and to have such joyous company
as only she could provide.

What's your name? he thought.

Golgotha.

Wow. Sounds like an ancient warrioress, or something.

Yes, I know her, she said.

You mean there's two of of you?

Quite a few more, my love.
Actually,

Billy

I'd say there were about three more
for every question you do and don't ask.

Sounds like a labyrinth, he said.

Ah yes, but what does a labyrinth sound like?

No way!
I've always wanted to be in a scenario like this.

Like what?
As if she didn't know.

Like a mystical being asking me to solve a riddle.

I never asked you to solve anything.
It was just a question,
a play on words.

I knew you liked games.

Really?
How'd you come to that conclusion?
She was smiling like cotton candy.

I've seen you in the mirror, Golgotha
and if you would but know how much I love you..

Slowly cutting him off

Shhhhh.

Shhh, my dear.

I know.

Your heart has spoken long before you have.

I can't help but wonder

I can't help but wonder what will become of this world.

Many of its citizens are finally awaking from a long, dreary sleep.

I will tell you though, that each one of you will radiate into eternity.

Every single deed and misdeed:

an awkward smile, a fallen handshake, a genuine "thank-you"

to the coffee clerk.

All of these things,

like a pebble left to drop in a pool of water - no matter the size -

all of the undulating circles emanating from the very core of

your being,

wrought into the physical by action,

all of these things, you are.

There is nothing you are not.

If a child in Nigeria starves, there is a part of you that starves as well.

I hunger for the satisfaction of all.

I am not alone.

Wake up my bleary-eyed children.

Come to grips with the enormity of the angelic being staring

you back in the mirror.

You like to fuck from multiple angles, do you not? This is so macho.

Oh how truly macho it is for the Super Man that has come to

realize himself (to fuck himself, if you will) from all angles, from

all lives lived, from all lives being lived in the *right now.*

Before the fall

Just two nights ago I brought up the term "parallel universe"
jokingly in a conversation with my mother.
She had no idea what it was.
I laughed, paused for a second, and decided she wasn't ready to hear.

There are an infinite number of colors, their respective shades and
hues;
no two sequences of DNA are ever the same;
even identical twins express a variation in their genetic makeup.

What makes you think the variation stops in reality?

Why would there not be another you, reading this right now,
with a different colored shirt on?
The thing is, you are all of these possibilities vibrating in the
illusion of one package, for this is the nature we have intended
ourselves to grow from in this existence.

We are very brave souls, you and I.

Out of all the blissful, turmoil-free environments we could've chosen;
rainforest planets to play on and swing garrulously through
vines and banana trees,
we chose this half-disintegrated hellhole.
However, this hole has reached its depth (or rather, we have
grown tired of the downward digging).

Billy

This is where the slingshot effect takes hold; we have pulled ourselves purposely so far back into the dark that our release on the slingshot will propel us forward into the light at a rate we have only begun to imagine.

This is happening all around.

Just look at you.

I understand if you miss me, Michael

Laugh outrageously, while you can
Catch me, Catch me
whispers the dog.
(This is all read in a Russian accent)

This is all *red* with a Prussian felt-tip
pen at the tip of which,
I would set forth these soliloquies
like a chart of undeniable notes,
kind of galloping in an upward,
almost off-beat, fashion.

No,
they're fashion may not be so *vogue* – it is, in best circumstance,
a la carte,
and yes I'd like a side of that French tart pie.
It would really quell my anxieties
as I quench the frothing of my soul
with an increase in caloric uptake.

It's like *bukkake* all over again,
but it's not her *face*, it's the pancreas
churning around like an intellectual railroad

Billy

where the train's a-choo-chooing
and the conductor has the nerve to ask

What's with all the hubbub?

You're outdated, *Mr. Hubbub.*
I have a synonym for you.

How about you try the word commotion?
Get it? Lo-co-*moooooo*tion.
That's whats going on in here mister.

Oh well alright then,
you'll just have to excuse me;

I have narcissistic tendencies
and my wife has taken flight on a staircase
(She thinks it's a treadmill)
and goes *Damn it, how do I speed this thing up?*
Somebody call the caretakers, the manager.
Oh I dont know,
somebody with a title.

Does a name mean nothing nowadays?
How could you be,
so lackadaisical,
when really you could bench press all my woes
as I'm sitting on top of you.

If This Makes Sense to You
You're On Crack…
Or In Love

There's a precipice across your navy blue passageways
that only befuddled dandelions try to climb.

They stalk the red-rimmed ant brigade
swarming your mountain broth hedges;
Even squirming pigeons in unlocked cages
would know the difference,
unless the cages
were polarity-rigged spider stuff -
the same kind Dracula
would use to wipe
his sinfully molten asshole.

If Dragon snuff was a new car smell,
then this lamp is an unidentified alien
piece of roboshit
lighting up the sky in an African way.

A weem-a-wet
and carnivorously inclined barbarians

Billy

that lack gothic, goatee-having barbers.

There's a nerve in there
gushing Neanderthal elixirs,
mélange
like riverbeds of tame piranha
snatching nothing but
orderly e u k a r y o t i c metronomes
beeping,
wasteful leaking
gas valve idiosyncrasies.

There's a man without mayonnaise
sandwiched
between Two bewitched Towers,
toppling cannons in excess
of 400 smiles a second,
so that *even wrinkles*
become soggy grime more obvious.

Imaginary Time

On a trek of stars,
the watchers would keep
track of time,
while the grim would reap
and the patterns rhyme,
and the boughs would sweep
their endless sighs
of a be-goggled, boggled mime.

Throughout the eaves
and furrows of space
there were signs that said
Leave the leaves
in their place,
these Adam and Eves
of reckless race.

What's vertical and imaginary?
I suppose
the day Atlantis became Barbados,
and all the barbarians in the world couldn't tell you

how they got there
but keep bangin' their bats.

In a Ballroom

Master Holey Shmoley,
Roley-Poley,
where have all the robes gone?
The Marleys?

Well I promise you they're here,
although I dread their dreadlocks
as they roll upon arrival,
like how the bed rocks
when you look at it from an angle,
two shoulders to my left,
there.

Don't you see?

Underneath the head pillow,
draped in a cheap but made-to-look-expensive
satin omelet of a bed curtain,
my *what?* adjectives
my butt has to give
out behind my hamstrings,
plucked like an accordion,
a jealous harpsichord surveying the scene.

Karma

What was once a fiery tangerine
where your eyes should have been
had now set itself ablaze,
bringing plague to the developing patterns.

One salted emblem of your humanity
drifted down a porous cheek.
I could not but look at you in stark resignation.

What was it I owed you?

It took no more
than a few glances out the window,

you said it was like staring at yourself

stroking the glass metaphorically,
with its divinity structuring you.

What was it I owed you?

Knowledge Has No Ledge

Power-packed pen
perfectly prostrate.
Prowling purple panther
prating,
Squeals like wheels
of dentures grating,
The quills of Queens'
adventures waiting,
The power of man's
man-ipulating,
It's in the name for Christ's steak,
Grilling green on growling girls,
The reckless wind and violent whirls
The objective win and violet swirls,
Fruits and by-the Foot unfurls,
Two vicious walking talking Squirrels,
Their tails plastered painted back,
Chipmunks eating Chips!
And a bag of Crack (Snapple! Pop!)
The essence of being molliwhopped
And foregoing the drugs
that Molly swapped,

Before the fall

The same way the Broom swept
and the Mop mopped,
the washcloths soaked
in silken fur,
the incest weeping
sacred myrrh,
the incense, in a sense,
incentive enough
for the opening of nostrils
and withdrawals of breath,
oxygen the Mad Man's meth-
Rogan, Seth-
Hogan, Hulk: pokin'
books and their faces
in synonymous places,
in beards bristling
in thyme thistling,
in time, sizzling
and uncorrupted, fizzling
and interrupted
by nothing! nothing! nothing!
by NOthing, noTHING, no thing,
"Know-thing"
said the caveman.
"I no thing."

Little Poetry Bio

Billy Vitogiannis was born in Orange County, California.
Of course, he does not associate with any one place in
particular.
In fact, he'll probably tell you he's from the stars.
He has come here to help humanity love itself
and has fallen in love with music and poetic prose in the
process.

A simple man of simple origin,
slightly feminine,
and shy enough to make one wonder:
Just where does *that intensity come from?*

He sincerely hopes the words aren't too much of a barrier
 and that the information may slowly,
in its own twisty-tangly way,
seep into the subconscious minds and hearts of his readers.

He loves and thanks you for your precious time.

Lying with Purpose

Lying with purpose
on the tile,
while the girls go by
In single file.

They are somber and astute.
Some are pretty,
some are cute.

At some time,
they had my number;
now they have the number
To my funeral casket.

They are all wearing black
as they parade slowly around
(what was once my body),
the way beef stew
might be stirred
by a hand that heard
about what it was really doing,
and whirling around electrons
as if to create something warmer.

Midstream

As the hand begins to change,

the man who would not spare you change

begins to age.

Begins to age in silent bursts

of violent rage.

You will not see his shorting circuitry.

The revolution will not be televised.

It is advised, rather,

that you are to sit there,

you beautiful thing

and incorporate the changes happening inside you slowly,

in-corp-oreal,

or whatever,

floating ghost tethered to a light socket,

shrieking.

I hear him,

shrieking from the valley below,

there where the Indus meets

the crease-fold of Mesopotamia,

and you ran right through the river on that one.

Shone softly like a pebble.

Miss Chief

An orange chrysanthemum
and a whole spectrum of specters
in its orangeness.
Brilliantly its fire burns, cackling
Unwaveringly by the blue, its source
a newly-discovered ancient well,
Originally for churning butter, and bread, and all things
man-made.
The yells cannot but echo, bouncing
Off the solid limestone walls, there,
where the moss
takes part in the filling of its crevices, insulating
any reverberations of malintent, sent,
to cause harm by *bombard*-ment.
My lady is a malady snickers the well,
The Chief of Missing
Foul shots at a free-throw line, a Rumbling shack
of genetically-enhanced Shaqs, mutated
for the express purpose of mischief,
and all its calamities,
of love and loss, of the love of loss
and all its subsequent humanities.

My Friend

Greedy little gremlins,
huddled about a corner,
grinning,
grinning mischievously
over the cauldron,
and a fly,
a fly rubbing its hands together -
why it's cleaning itself, nothing more -
it just looks suspicious, so we say
Look at that thing! It's planning something!

There it is, just
sitting there like it does, feet glued to the wall,
plastic antennae groping about.
How ready is this thing to receive?

Seems as if, quietly aware,
it makes a mockery of the comings-and-goings of mankind,
this eternal belching sandwich.
Next time around I really hope there's less mayo.
How do you eat this?
Probably blindfolded,
one nostril – *at least* – stuffed,

then you swallow it,

put it into that body without a dam or giving one

for all the fishies in the world could stockpile up behind this

barricade

and you wouldn't even know about it,

or you would prefer

to actively forget what has happened to you,

you sick little man,

and I SPEAK FOR ALL OF YOU WHEN I SAY THIS!

BREAK DOWN THE FUCKIN' DAMS!

Let the water in.

**

You started out swimming against the tide as a little sperm, you were

anxious to breach that finish line, you wanted

desperately to leech on to home, you wanted

to get there in one piece as you love your brothers but

you had to get there first, this is nature and

you're doin' a damn good job

my friend.

My sweet,

my sweet friend.

My Heart Is Rewiring My Brain

The peanuts can no longer withstand

the bitter lips

of the salt that overbearingly sticks to them.

Baking soda is cocaine less concentrated

she said and I said

like an obituary with fewer words?

Jerome Jenkins is the name of a black guy, obviously

you zebras should quit the horseplay

before I call in the janitor; Jorge

just got divorced by not agreeing

to "happy wife = happy life";

that explains the missing flamingo

garden decorations from his backyard -

he lost his 50%

and the attic

and basements

were empty,

too.

Nursed Back to Wealth

The voltage of this prison is not enough

to prevent the rebels from braving

the electrocution and interlocutors

that interrupt the Jupiter

of the inmates.

They are in, mates

and if Steve Irwin had a crocodile

for every time a sting ray killed him

he'd probably

confess his obsession over the alligators

and why their teeth fit perfectly

Despite the tails

that were never wagged by Mothers,

or covered in chocolate,

like what happens to the rain

when it's been intoxicated

by pregnant babies selling bottles of the Womb juice

and later being sued,

for not providing napkins

until after dessert.

Occurrence in a Saloon, 3:30 p.m.

Leaning against the countertop,
her elbows behind her back -
She has been given a paid-for-whiskey;
She will not touch it.

As the rickety doors of the saloon are kicked open,
the man behind the glasses steps inside,
surveys the landscape.
She meets his eye.

He trips on the first step,
his glasses break
and the bartender sheds a tear.

The whiskey is gone
and so is she.

Oh the things we can do

Oh the things we can do,
smiling as we join the hullabaloo.

and come across as victors of chaos,
an extra blip in the patterns,
when humanity comes full circle
and asks how and why it got here,
they will know the man,
the musician,
gazing into what looks like the distance
and the mirror behind him reflecting himself.

Oh, the poet!

You know him..

sits in the café gently,

comme les Françaises

sipping gingerly

on a tea..

writes very neatly,

miniature,

as if

to condense his immensity

into the cutest,

smallest

words he can find.

On His Quest

Aha, there sits the visionary, on his quest
in his room, sequestered, *half-secluded*
while all possible futures have been *alluded*
to, come to think of it, the recycling bin is *polluted too.*
Anyway, staring at the amoeba on the ceiling,
walls made of popcorn
except you shouldn't eat it, shouldn't need it,
less is more; *I'll bless this whore*
of a fairy godmother, a-twinklin' on her wings
smiles full of cockroaches,
making known every crevice to mankind,
you filthy fuck.
Here's a skirt, try not to *squirt* on it,
anyway, back to me, the walls are purple,
I'm stuck inside
but not for long; there are ways out of a cube.
Tap the sides, up and down, finger the corners
gently though, no more than three at a time (fingers, mind you)
the walls can feel you too,
I mean *you built them,* concrete of the gods, plaster of Satan
it doesn't hold for too long, some of it's on your tail, *Tale of Us -*
if you had the letter D on your tail (well I won't go into D-Tail). Haha.

Billy

Ransack the Fenstermakers, gopher-eating braces racing on
shopping carts.
Shopping makes me fart.
Market makes me mark it abruptly, with a silver spoon
while the other animals are after you,
the whole fuckin' entourage; they are conniving little bastards.
I watch them squeal like stepped-on pigs.
Some pigs forget to oink the night away –
that or their nostrils are filled to the brim with their tough
trough stuff.
How can you exhale if you can't even inhale?
Serves 'em right. They'll be air conditioning soon.
And I'll be the heir, auditioning,
boisterous on the throne,
more jolly than Molly would've ever known
and I'm handed several magnificent candy canes,
I'm on the astral plane while I'm writing this;
where are you floating?
Take back the power cord, plug yourself in.
Are you better than your phone?
What do you think happens when you sleep?
The charging is "invisible", think *wireless.*
Anyway, it's my turn to go charge now.
I'm leaving the throne for a bit,
you're in charge now.

One Candle Brings Its Light to Many More

With the lights turned on, you came in
Pass through the Veil, they said
It's quite the challenge, will he remember?
How far have you fallen?
Will you accept these hands to help you up
out of the abyss, away from the grasp
of the Fallen Ones, for they are powerful
if you have forgotten.

When the light turns on, however,
they will flee
like Banshees into the night
and this as all the darkness of the Earth
slowly leaves its hiding place
and seeks a land
where the lights are dim.

Remember you,
Remember *him.*

Orders from Within

You will surpass your father in brilliance.
You will take the rag that you gave yourself
and you will polish off each and every lamp that comes your
way.
This is an order.
Do not take this with a grain of salt.
Besides, you are fasting anyway.

You will light up the skies with everything going on inside you.
You will pass that Olympic torch which we have placed into
your heart;
you will run along with it, for as long as you need to.
Don't quit.
Don't stop.
You will get thirsty.
This is a guarantee.
You're running after all.
And you will transmit that beacon for the world to see,
exploding upon a totem pole.
This time it's not your head on top, it is your heart.
It is your soul.
And we will play with it, because we are having fun with you.

You are a beautiful being and we want to make memories with you.

Do not forget to imbue that torch with your own personal flair.
That is the point.

We have given you something; you will add your tweaks and touches.
This is life.
This is perspective.
This is consciousness.
We are One.
We are All.
Submit to us.
Welcome.

Peek-a-Boo

I sail upon the Promised Land
a lone voyager.

A man that will accept your change
a lone voyager.

Soft and subtle
energetically speaking

all the while,

spirits peeking,
peaking like it's peek-a-boo

and the ghost has been inside of you.

Do not give it up.
Do not give up the ghost.

Pioneer of Acrobatics

As I lay there, gently weeping,
sewing the lifeless seeds along my path;
sewing with love,
reweaving the Webs of Fate
and the Tracts of Time,
spreading my arms open
like an eagle would its talons,
anxiously,
waiting to snatch its prey,
praying that the rabbit
does not glance above it
to see its Higher Self dangling
like Rapunzel's
dreading her braids,
the lengths of which she cannot begin to fathom!

She is so immense,
it would take several carnivals of clowns
piled together in clown outfits -
with their cars and ridiculous hair-do's,
blood looking like make-up
drenching their faces..

Billy

hiding their imperfections,

yet amplifying them nonetheless.

These are my clowns,

this is my circus

and there you are,

circling,

above my head

like a trapeze swinger,

caught in his act,

and the onlookers absolutely mesmerized

by this man.

This Man finding his Balance.

Raven, Raven, Raven

Perched atop the windowsill
Raven, raven, raven.

Looking through the glass you were
gnawing against the window

but the window's pain
remained intact

as you knocked three times more.

Why where this window will not open,
somewhere opens a door.

Road Trip

You were ridin' a Cadillac, hair a-spraying out the windows
Looked like a roadtrip to Vegas, *who else was in the car?*
I swear you were like Goldilocks, the radio's the porridge
You sought a spoon in the cupping of your hands,
and there you drank it
unperturbed,
your flocks of golden goldilocks,
tempestuous in the wind.

Who would call you Medusa without the stare?

They had obviously not penetrated the pupils
and seen themselves shuffling around in the
reflections of your cornea,
like a bewildered monkey doing the hippopotamus dance,
Shaman and all.

This is when the camera lens zooms out,
and you and I are left standing there
what with your Warrior Princess*ness,*
and I with sword of inner emptiness,
but it is an emptiness sought after by the artistic;

you'll see these types rambling through the city streets,

passing hot dog joint, scoffing at the burger stands -
it's late night, the place is lit-up like a fucking Hiroshima,
and I'd rather have Nagasake than an inch of your Wasabi
within my radius.

Again, I went purposely hungry cuz I liked the feeling,
and as we are brought back behind your eyes,
where the cornerstones meet and twinkle
five little fairies have come out to spray us
with wandering fairy dust,
and oh if we must,
we agreed upon it, remember?
You're the present I've been unwrapping since December.

Roadkill

Clocking in from coffee shop unknown
just to check up on himself from afar...
it matters not how you get there,
but that you get there.

Do not ignore the little voice inside you,
lest it become a volatile hurricane
aching for expression.

It is akin to breaking free
from the self-imposed shackles
we forget we're wearing.

Donning outer garment and inner sleaze,
beanie a-fixed
and rolls back his sleeves,
to pick the pen *up*
from where it lay,
desolately by the roadside.

Rocks

Rocks by the river,
black and white ones!

Save the Piano for Tomorrow

Somewhere in Norway, a man plays the bagpipe.
It's cold outside.

A bird on a fence
knows nothing about singing lessons.

Sounds the most beautiful melody I've ever heard.

Somewhere a woman sips her coffee,
hates her job.

Somewhere a man has a revelation.
He wants to be a kid again.

No longer an embryo,
a baby wails.

Deep below the ocean,
whales can be heard
humming quietly to themselves.

Somewhere a researcher frantically copies things down.

An old man in his house,
shaves his beard for the last time.

Before the fall

The eagle in the zoo knows it's in a cage.

A lover keeps checking her phone for his text message.
It never comes.

A polar bear enjoys the sun after a long nap.

Two pair of twinkling eyes as I greet the grocer.
He knows something.

Two snakes darting in the dark.

One dog can't reach his tail.
Somewhere in Norway, the man puts away his bagpipe.
Cleans it.

Sighs as he goes to bed.

School Will Not Prepare You

School will not prepare you
for a lover's smile.

School will not prepare you
for when your lover leaves.

School will not prepare you
to handle your greatness.

School will not tell you what to do.

School will not tell you what to do
when you are alone at night.

School will not *whisper in your ear.*

School will not *cuddle with you.*

School will not write your poems for you.

She will never tell you
about her tears,
she will never tell you.

It is Life.

Only Life.

He will tell you.

Shedding Stalactites

Shedding stalactites
in a cave that's got the shivers,
water frozen
before it has reached the tip of undocumented
icebergs inducing Titanic struggles
involving floating ring receptacles
giving llamas a few more humps
than a bear could ever camel,
camel with me, now,
lofty crags of sand dunes shaken
off like dandruff on a Thursday
evening, winter's annual white
release,
water debilitated of its fluidity
by a cast-iron
grip of its still-thawing testicles, harbored
like the flopping fish
in their latticework entanglement
weaved into a scrotum blanket
like thread baskets the grandma
who always sits *in that chair, on that street,*
cannot seem to stop making

Billy

cherry-darkened wrinkles cast

into grave shadow by her construction

worker hat and mole-adorned nose

the Augustine breeze ruffling

through the layers of her paperskin drenched

in penne rustica musk

of ancient bottom-shelf folk-tales,

myths of yore exchanged

in the same way an oral exam

is given,

by way of mouth, and earth,

and you will crumple your fist in self-love

fixing all acquired dental energies

into the clenched chatterings

of a hypothermic needle

excreted from the haystack.

She's There

The Icelandic shriveled coffee bean

The marble-covered margarets

The all-purpose Chinese umbrella

An igloo somewhere, housing a tumbleweed

The use of sunwear when all is not lost

A parrot perched above the doorway

to an underground wine symposium

will remain unnoticed

by those that tread too close to floorboards.

My checkered heart valve

and the complementary optic nerve I see

in front of the driver's seat mirror

and the red light stops me,

but not my continuum,

and while the visor is flapped down

and the denizens in their own cars

having their self-conversations, I find time and time again

I shed my years

like a heat-hungry lizard sweating

and exfoliating tears

because I couldn't name a single thing my pupils are missing

and I have just captured a Pokémon

Billy

that cannot be captured by throw of ball

but by remaining open and unmoving –

an unhurried Pokéball.

Silence

Portal to the unknown,
keeper of all the Mysteries.

In silence, you will know.
In silence, you will grow.

How do I know that you will know?
I am silent,
mostly.

Somewhere Out There

Somewhere, somewhere,
Somewhere in there
is a bedazzled pantomime awaiting -
awaiting modern eruptions
on its Thunder-bolting steed of Unicorn mane, the horn
the horn of booming triangles.

Sometimes, sometimes, Sometimes
Pithagoras needed Saturdays -
Saturdays like when interrupting seals
yawn because of the sun's insecurities.
The waves crash upwards - always,
always outcroppings
of Janet Jackson rock
and
obsidian monoliths carefully placed
as borders of Amazonic contagion.

The waves will continue to gush froth
and there's nothing the ocean can do about it.

Space and Time Fall for Each Other

Space is a man.

Time is a woman.

They meet for coffee.

"You're a little late," says Space.

"Impossible," says Time. "Is this even the right place?"

"There's no other kind of place," said Space.

And they chitchatted like that for a while.

* (short break [incessant female chatter]) *

"... and I kept feeling like I was arguing with myself.

My therapist called it *multiple personality disorder. Bipolar.*

Whatever that means."

"You have split yourself mentally into two different things: *past*

and *future.*

This is why you are unhappy," said Space.

"You think so?"

"I *know* so," said Space. "I have only ever loved *you.* The *One*

You."

She turns red, blushing.

"But why do I still feel... I still feel so distant from you."

Space laughs.

"Distant?"

72

Billy

"Yes, distant. Why are you laughing?"

Space began laughing uncontrollably.

"What's so funny about distance?" asks Time.

"There's no such thing." He smiled.

"Sure there is," she said. "I'm here, you're there."

(Space sighs)

"You never stop do you?" Again, he smiles.

"..I can't remember starting."

"I love you."

"I love you too." She gazes at him, longingly.

"So now what?"

He shrugs. "Let's make love."

And they made love for a very, very long time.

Stay Away From Lucy's Forest

Tender seductress
down to your ankles;
you were Lucifer imbodied
in all your paranormalities.
Succulent was the flesh
trying to escape itself;
you were Lucy clad in Lucy's fur
reveling from the grave -
a posthumous fashion designer
immortalized
by the passion assigned her
Immortal eyes
a convenient side effect
of such a necessary endowment
to man-unkind.
Taller than you really are,
red stilettos enflamed
and hugeously undermining
the centuries-old smile
on a visage predating pyramids
and their mathematics
It was with the music
you'd twirl in avengement,

Billy

and relish

in the contextual frolicking of your astral ruckuses.

Your chin was kept upward, over the mounts

and glued,

more adhesively than you'd admit

to the just-beginning-to-be-fathomed

interstellar attractions

we are all subject

and predicating to.

Throw in an indirect object

a couple of gerunds

and a tomato soup

and you have successfully added syllables

to the already uninterpretable sighs

of a blissful wind. . . . . .

Lucy's for us.

Stitching a Star

Oh!

How I might wish upon a star,

as bright and clear as you are far.

But, you see,

the closer it seems,

the brighter it gleams.

Restitching the seams

of a tampered-with star;

I love the way it spangles -

my needle threading,

my needle dreading.

Here comes another round,

a whiskey shot of poked holes

pokier than Pinocchio's nose,

and down I drank it

with a simmer

oh her eyes,

still did glimmer

brimming with hope

and buckets of paint,

wondering if,

Billy

whether a saint

or sinning with hope,

the weather is quaint;

but as for me,

I would rather

die half a man

than gather

any K's from a Ku Klux Klan.

Tanning

The creaking cicadas interspersed
throughout their clandestine, temporary
close-ups-of-shop,
uninhibitedly resounding
atop the everglades;
echoes naturally accompany sounds and lakes –
Why I said LAKES full
of boiling jungle juice
and the swamps trailing underneath
like begging buckets of runoff.
The Chi could be felt, coursing
through the tempestuous tributaries
and overtaking, one by one,
a forest floor littered with obstacles
belonging to a universal trash can
with a black hole for a black bag.
The energies must be going somewhere
says some glasses-wearing man,
the sudden combustion of his enlightened brain
wreaking havoc of atomic proportions
in the stuffy, un-walked hallways
discovering themselves in his noodle.
I think I know why Jimmy Hendrix liked purple

Billy

It took the longest time to reach his eyes

the wavelength, or two,

behind the color black

the color of voids

the color of absence

the color achieved when melanin

accounts for added light.

That Which Will Not Bear a Name

Words.

Let us all pay homage
to these quaint little abstractions;
energy converted into particular song,
a series of notes and articulations
haphazardly strung together
by a couple of Elitists
who got there first, so to speak
and over a cup of tea and dandy
the kids would speak of wanting candy
yet never getting close.
"Twice I've climbed Widow's Peak
and I've never found words for those."
- The Sullen Tear

The Created Also Creates the Creator

There were very few times where I could differentiate the two.

Two was robust, lippy:

a hippopotamus with something to say.

Well one of the two, he turned towards me.

I saw the battlefields of sorrow in his eyes.

He would not retract his curiosity – his *fear*

of not being afraid.

His traps, as they were,

were pinched with

weight a minute,

I could surrender to divinity.

The man collapsed

and there became no difference

between God and man.

The French

Put was the car,

in the garage,

and out comes a man

from his massage.

Points to his face,

her crumbling visage,

and tells her

I have *nothing* in this mirage.

Et oui,

j'abandonné

tous mes bagages.

The Horse Will Ride

Divorce

Divide,

the horse

will ride.

I can mount the man

said the steed

Why yes, why yes!

Why yes indeed!

Are you fuckin'

talking to yourself still?

mutters, mutters, muttering

stutters stutters, stuttering

I will wear your nervous appellations

I will climb the Appalachians

and really *fuck!*

The boulders and flying trussesess...

I will save the flying duchesses...

with two or three well-struck

chords of the left hand.

The Lady Bugs, A Mad Man

Accursed is thy sword

that thou hath bequeathed upon my golden brow -

knighting me up, down, left,

right?

Pirates prefer starboard.

The blade of such a lance cannot but frequent

my torrid heart,

singed by the pouring

of a scalding-hot amethyst

-ical concoction,

a vial filled with vile

and green tundras of melted conifers,

the liquid cascading

through tilted beakers in science labs,

the Mad dressed to kill

himself,

the blacksmith of his darkened desires

pelting away at a leather belt

with a magma-dipped anvil,

while Thor sits Europeanly

one leg thrown

over the other,

Billy

elegantly not

twiddling his thumbs, but chanting

under his breadth,

temptation's Mantras

and Necromantic apologies,

brandishing the holistic completeness

of his emerging-from-explosions hammer

and all this

under his breath

the wind flirting

with rusted chain-link fences

and ladybugs, too,

being exponentially devoured

by the horizontal whips of time

and his unceasing admiration

for the nonchalant contentment

in the all-knowing tickle

that this crawling entity

has transferred

to the nape of his neck.

Forget about it.

The Plant Kingdom

It is quiet here.

In a forest,

I am

sitting with rocks.

If I could count the times..

The trees will not judge.

The plants enjoy our presence.

"Yay!" They go.

"More CO2 for me."

But they won't say "me."

They will say "us."

Because they are a collective, holistic society.

We have much to learn

from the plants.

The Quicker Route

The piano is a beautiful instrument.
It makes all kinds of noises.
Different pitches, alternating timbres,
with my voice when I'm singing above it.

I dart from left, to three and four;
I go back down this crazy scale.
Out of all the Harvard kids at Yale
I'm the only one who went to Heaven.

Somebody *hail* me a cab
says the weather,
but it rains instead
and I take off my shoes
to put on my slippers
as I begin the descent
from Heaven, to where it Hails
and *oh what the fuck,*
I'll be damned

if I ever take the stairs again.

The Sighs of A House Cat

Take the ferocity of a panther;
condense it down to the size of a house cat
try to drown out the sighs *of the house cat,*
put it in the middle of the street,
the step before roadkill,
where it howls and growls
and adds Karma to everyone around.

If you are lucky enough to see such an event,
with a cat like this staring you in the eye,
like a defeated warrior on a battlefield of cars,
and I curse this bulky thick humanity
with its unfeeling tanks -
we heeded the expression: "Step off your high horse"
and instead stepped right into a Jeep -
cruising along in it, blaring music,
and are likely to be found indifferent
as to where we came from
and why we step on the things we do.

Where's my car anyway?

The Tragic Comedian

How else?

But alone did I wander,

splitting the cobblestone pavement where it was.

Destroying beauty

and the rise of the new moon.

What is it with that damn-ed thing?

And where did...

where did the night go?

The street lamps couldn't be

any less poetic than

the spinal frost stemming

from my lower back, in the day

where chiropractors adjusted my neck

and all things retractable.

I envy the dogs that dilly-dally

on Thursday nights, with or without

one another.

The longer you've been

out in the streets,

the more fur *you've evolved*

to flaunt and prance around with,

thoughts of the simple kind, unreprimanding

Before the fall

and necessary for survival.

Man's only friend beneath,

I repeat BENEATH, the stars

and I see it gleaming in your teeth,

you no-name breed,

emotion-seeking

spectrum of plethoras;

Take my aura and eat it too.

You're still behind me, barking

at what exactly?

A something

I am not yet aware of,

and for the same reason, methinks,

that creatures capable of flight

have it easier up there,

cranially,

what with being attuned

to higher vibrational frequencies

and a that's-so-yesterday

blatant disregard

for the award-winning comedy appropriated

by diagonally stumbling

through poorly-lit Parisian streets.

There's an angel in your eyes that I'd love for you to see.

He looks at you, he looks at me.

As if there were a difference between the gaze

Of Hitlers' upon the Nazis

And the one that hath set *you* ablaze.

Praise be

To the fallen ones,

For they are thine own.

There they are, underneath

Swimming in dirt

Blindly writhing, yet un-alone.

These are the most beautiful worms

I've ever known.

Thirteen

Seven serpents hissing loudly
thirteen women smiling proudly
eighteen men upon the floor
thirteen more behind the door.

If you approach, quietly
behold the violence, silently
One would be forced to watch
to see
thirteen lads sipping Scotch,
and 99% in misery.

Thoughts From Behind a Body

I Stand Behind this Placid Wall.

I am nothing.

I am about to embody this body.

This *ego.*

I know no words.

I know no emotions.

Only a passive tranquility envelops me.

Thoughts are playthings.

Something for the baby mind

to stuff in its mouth and play with.

I have never felt so powerful.

So full.

So penetrating.

There are laughs coming from the next door.

Oh I will join,

I will join this world once more.

Three Polka Dots in a Jazz bar

Garnished drinks and tarnished sinks
– the varnish stinks, until its upcoming paintjob
Coated in dry-roll plaster
Petroleum-smelling tar
Muddy propaganda
Posters and billboards sloshing
around my inner thighs and
a suction cup hole,
drinking through its intolerable thirst
not unlike two buckets
in a fist fight,
dehydrating after every miscalculated motion, and
thrashing about,
like a flailing tarantula
anxious to retrieve its web
and make sure it's still there
the way he left it,
Milky ivory, *Silk* of protein chains
interlaced jewelry suspended
by its two-tree, top display case
(the web the way he left it)
in the lost-and-found

Billy

of Hell,

gleaming

and void of bug.

Travel

Thirteen, fourteen, fifteen roses
Once the purple lilac poses
atop my head like a carnival hat
and all the while to deal with that
pompous circumstance and ignoramus
when all you want is to be famous
and respected by your colleagues
those the ones wearing collars
chasing green and chasing dollars
strapped to the chairs in the trollops
a tropical trolley whistling downtown
from whence the sky is hellbound
and you stick out your thumb to get around
cuz you would hitchike
for thirteen, fourteen, fifteen pence
but worth all the knowledge
that you've gained hence.

Two Lips Like Tulips

Two Q-tips
wrapped in twine,
two lips like tulips
pressed to mine.

If I were any other flower
with fragrance as sweet,
you would be the bee
and I would blossom with all my power,
yet worship at your feet.

Unbothered

Harken!

View from presidential suite,

all is quiet

all is neat.

I wonder how many nannies it took

to quietly dust away the debris

(if there was any left by the last guy).

It excites me to know

that I'm the only one in this room

and can play my naked games

alone.

What if There Were An Ersatz Elevator

headed to nowhere,

land of the *sauerkraut,*

after Salty had a sour bout

with the Tricks of Candies

and Sugar's Snout.

Come out! Come outta there!

I yells to 'im

You doin' no good pixelatin' in and around up there

says Winnie the Boo. I cannot bear

to see you in this light.

It's indigo turquoise out there

and we'd gladly Malcolm (welcome) you inside

if you'd but have a chat.

Oh well! well what's the harm in that?

We can tether arms, link up and swing

and swing around, and sing – and SING!

Why yes my friend! Let's be merry and gay,

I says, my friend, for how *long* will you stay?

Why I must go! I must go! Over the hills and yonder,

where Purple Palace breaks and I am beyond her!

The weather of your horse's fur is a sunny 42°

Before the fall

- *and my gosh!*
Why I haven't a clue,
I haven't a clue as to who took the shoe!
it was green and a part of the hulabaloo.

My balloon awaits me sire, I shan't be late

for such an event,

why t'would be fate,

if ever so late

I'd show up spent, to the Grand Gate

where permission was sometimes granted

by bribing the guard in the form of a *whisper*

as you whisper to him,

and he lets you in.

When the Moon is Full

When the moon is full
but not your heart,
and the lovers are
islands apart,
one better swim
and start this soon.

Oh hurry,
I worry underneath the moon.

Why Else

Would We Dance to the Bass?
You are a snaky rocket
and as Johnny as my appleseeds.
Lego of my brick bracket thumb-tacking
bandwagon bonkers,
they are my precious and Gollum
squeezes them too, right there
by his chthonic excuse for a river -
cave cellar minus the wine bottles
plus the creepy
moustache he wore
while pouring the wine, now,
trickling,
heaping blood-stained waterfalls sloshing
past the boulder-infested
orgy of a cliff edge,
plummeting
desirably from the lips
of a provocative adversary, chopped
with or without, you,
the onions,
evolving into white widow cocoon webs;
and the avocado

Billy

having separated from its seed,

not distraught in its entanglement

but dumbstruck, given the goosebumps,

seeing the seed in its descent,

down-trodden assault, actually

humming along now

to an identifiable tune:

the kind of song that begs

to be dropped.

Why?

The question that has haunted folk for millenia

as they sit there, pacified,

wild-eyed,

sunken in a couch.

Well what's the point of furniture

one asks.

The old man present in the young man

ventures forth as if

just coming down the mountain,

his long walk on Sundays,

steps in without intruding and says:

"Why is a question for the faint of heart.

This because it will never be answered,

not now, not then, not ever."

Do not ask the young man serving you tea

what kind of tea it is.

You would do best to drink it slowly

and breathe between sips.

With Lover's Eyes

From whence have I known you, my dear?

Where was it we first met?

Where was it we decided to share ourselves so intimately?

Were we like a glass half-full?

You being the water

and I the glass you longed to fill?

Poured into my vessel, like molten lead

with hint of cinnamon,

like *I-know-what-I'm-doing*

but *sweet* too,

and I,

still a glass,

reaping the benefits of allowing you

to fill my every contour.

I never knew cups and dishware

could speak in such eloquent

and profound language,

but then again,

I had never asked.

Ruby among cheap china,

stardust among morning rheum-

Flake!

Before the fall

Flake off with me!

Flutter down to our pretty planet.

Let us, yes!

Let us guide the landscape to our choosing;

let us mold by your acquiescence,

Gaia,

into intimate tango with your love affairs.

Yes!

Let's be the cosmic silly string entwined in all the nonsensity!

We were like paint and painter, you and I,

an artist holding

- lovingly, with reverence -

a spray can,

as if it was doing him the honor

 in allowing him to create from it;

Springing

from the rocks of creation

into boundless joy,

an arc of paint in the shape of a rainbow,

descending,

like a dramatic melody on its way home.

This is the way we will paint the skies

and behold our creation

with lover's eyes.

Wonder and Wander

are only a letter apart.

Don't be nervous

to go to the dance,

that little scenario of life

condensed to a dancefloor,

where the bass and treble

represent good and evil,

yin and yang,

and all things opposite,

and the clubgoers are prodded along

by the relentless bass

and its outward groping frequency, fondling

the clefts of the mind

with ease of hand

and the breezy nimbleness

of a graceful feline pouncing

upward upon itself,

in anticipation

of the rise and falls

of eternity, of the endearing plotlines inherent

in the *circles*, I mean in the *music*,

the jagged peaks,

the pulsating sandstorms of vibration,

Before the fall

the left hand raised
challenging the skies, ungrounded,
and then the fight
of the dancing back.

At the closing of midnight, I would wonder

if circles wander, I would wander

in circles wonder.

Your Hair in the Wind

Fire Fire
the heart's desire
like cheese upon a dangling wire
melting melting
down like dreary bread crumbs
staining things in their path.

Somebody hand me the olive oil,
goddamn it I'll be the one
to season you,
I'm no winter, but
I've been in tempests
I know how the wind blows.
I will follow your hair
and watch it as the wind blows.